Snap books®

Queens and Princesses

QUEEN
Christina
OF SWEDEN

by Joanne Mattern

Consultant:

Byron J. Nordstrom, PhD

Professor of History, Gustavus Adolphus College

St. Peter, Minnesota

Capstone press®

Mankato, Minnesota

Snap Books are published by Capstone Press,
151 Good Counsel Drive, P.O. Box 669, Mankato, Minnesota 56002.
www.capstonepress.com

Library of Congress Cataloging-in-Publication Data
Mattern, Joanne, 1963–
    Queen Christina of Sweden / by Joanne Mattern.
    p. cm. — (Snap books. Queens and princesses)
    Summary: "Describes the life and death of Queen Christina Vasa of Sweden"
— Provided by publisher.
    Includes bibliographical references and index.
    ISBN-13: 978-1-4296-2310-0
    ISBN-10: 1-4296-2310-1
    1. Christina, Queen of Sweden, 1626–1689 — Juvenile literature. 2. Queens
— Sweden — Biography — Juvenile literature. 3. Sweden — History — Christina,
1632–1654 — Juvenile literature. I. Title.
DL719.M38 2009
948.5'034092 — dc22   2008030113

Editor: Kathryn Clay
Book Designer: Bobbi J. Wyss
Illustrator: Abbey Fitzgerald
Set Designer: Juliette Peters
Photo Researcher: Wanda Winch

Essential content terms are **bold** and are defined at the bottom of the page where
they first appear.

1 2 3 4 5 6 14 13 12 11 10 09

Table of Contents

The Young
QUEEN

On a cold February day in 1633, 6-year-old Christina Vasa stood tall and proud at the front of a grand room. Around her were members of the Swedish **parliament** called the Riksdag. Noblemen, clergy, businessmen, and peasants stared at the young girl. All were there to honor the new queen of Sweden.

Christina wore her finest clothes. A long dress with big, puffy sleeves flowed around her tiny body. A large ruff covered her neck. She wore pointy, high-heeled shoes. Her hair fell over her shoulders. Jewels gleamed from her neck, arms, and fingers. Christina didn't like wearing these fancy clothes. She much preferred the comfort of her riding boots and pants.

Even though she was young, Christina knew that this was a very important day. She was pleased by all the attention she was given. Christina was just 6 years old, but she was the most important person in Sweden.

Christina, shown here at age 8, dressed up for special events, but she preferred to wear her riding clothes.

parliament — a group of people who make laws and run the government in some countries

Three months earlier Christina's father, King Gustavus II Adolphus, was killed at the Battle of Lutzen. When a Swedish king died, his son became the next ruler. If the king had no sons, another male relative became king. Gustavus Adolphus had no sons, but he wanted Christina to rule Sweden.

Before he went into battle, King Adolphus told the government his plan. He announced that Christina would succeed him and become queen. Until that time, Christina would be raised just like a prince. Her father chose a group of scholars and government officials to give her a good education. She would learn fighting, horseback riding, and all the skills boys learned. Most importantly, she would learn how to rule Sweden.

King Adolphus (center) swore his allegiance to his daughter in front of government leaders.

KING GUSTAVUS II ADOLPHUS
(1594–1632)

King Adolphus became the ruler of Sweden when he was 17 years old. He ruled for 21 years, until his death at Lutzen. During his reign, he led many successful battles. He also made a number of strong **alliances**. His sound military decisions made him very popular among the Swedish people.

His popularity helped Christina's claim to the throne. Many councilors worried about having a female ruler. But then they saw the family resemblance in the little girl's face. Her face convinced them that she would follow in her father's powerful footsteps.

A SURPRISING
Birth

Gustavus Adolphus' family had ruled Sweden for more than 100 years. Christina's mother, Maria Eleonora, was from Prussia, which is now part of Germany. Maria Eleonora didn't like living in Sweden. She thought it was a rough, uncivilized country compared to Germany. But Maria loved Gustavus Adolphus. She also loved being queen, so she made the best of her life in Sweden.

The harsh weather conditions of the country took their toll on the foreign queen. In her first few years of marriage, she had lost three children. Now she was pregnant for the fourth time. Gustavus Adolphus and Maria Eleonora hoped to have a son who would one day rule Sweden. They asked many fortune-tellers if their baby would be a boy or a girl. Every fortune-teller told the couple the baby would definitely be a boy. When Christina was born on December 8, 1626, everyone was very surprised.

Maria Eleonora was especially upset. She worried that she had disappointed her husband by giving birth to a girl. Gustavus Adolphus had a different idea. He was amused that all the fortune-tellers were wrong. He told everyone, "She will be a clever girl. She has already deceived all of us."

For Maria Eleonora, living in Sweden was a big adjustment.

A SUDDEN CHANGE

Like most royal children in the 1600s, Christina was not raised by her parents. Instead servants and special nurses took care of her. Christina saw her mother a few times a day. But it was the nurses who fed Christina, dressed her, changed her, and played with her. Christina also spent two years living with her aunt and uncle at Stegeborg Castle. Maria Eleonora was often away visiting her family or traveling with her husband.

As a result, Maria Eleonora never had a close relationship with her daughter. Gustavus Adolphus, however, adored Christina. And she equally loved her father. But their close relationship didn't last long.

Sweden had been fighting in the Thirty Years' War for many years. Christina's father was often away at battle. During one of these battles, Gustavus Adolphus was killed. It took several weeks for the news to reach Sweden. Upon hearing the news, Christina's life changed forever.

Gustavus Adolphus (center) was killed while fighting at the Battle of Lutzen.

THE THIRTY YEARS' WAR

The Thirty Years' War was fought from 1618 to 1648. Most of the battles took place in what is now Germany. The war began as a religious fight between Protestants and Catholics. In time, the war involved most major European countries. The war eventually became a fight for political control of Europe.

The conflict began when a Catholic nobleman named Ferdinand became king of Bohemia. Many Protestant leaders in Bohemia feared that a Catholic ruler would take away their religious rights. Several Bohemian noblemen tried to kill two of Ferdinand's messengers. This created a revolt. The war between the Protestants and Catholics spread across all of Europe.

Fighting continued for 30 years and destroyed Germany. More than half of its men were killed. Armies ruined crops and farmlands. Many people died from famine and disease. The war finally ended in 1648 with the Treaty of Westphalia.

3

A LONELY
Childhood

Christina's mother never got over her husband's death. After he died, she rarely left her room. She hung black curtains over the windows. Maria Eleonora kept the king's heart in a golden box over her bed. She often made Christina sleep in the same bed, beneath the container with her father's heart. On those nights, Christina lay terrified in bed.

Maria Eleonora paid little attention to Christina. When she did, it was usually to criticize her. Christina liked to play with swords, but her mother wanted her to play with dolls. Maria Eleonora tried to dress her daughter in fancy clothes and teach her to sew like other girls. Christina was not interested in these things. She preferred to chase after her dogs and spend hours riding horses. Her father had wanted her to be raised like a prince. That was also what Christina wanted.

Christina spent her days learning how to rule Sweden.

13

A ROYAL EDUCATION

Eventually Maria Eleonora's criticisms became too distracting to Christina's education. Christina was once again sent to live with her aunt and uncle at Stegeborg Castle. There she was treated kindly and received an excellent education.

While Christina enjoyed playing with her cousins, much of her time was spent studying. Some of the smartest people in Sweden came to instruct Christina. They taught her to speak German, French, Spanish, and Italian. She was also able to read and write in Latin.

Christina studied the history of Sweden and learned about the ancient Greeks and Romans. She studied philosophy, science, and mathematics. Christina was very proud of her education. She spent much of her life surrounding herself with scholars.

Christina spent most of her time studying at Stegeborg Castle.

AXEL OXENSTIERNA

When Christina first became queen, she was too young to actually rule Sweden. A group of **regents** made most of her decisions. The most important regent was a nobleman named Axel Oxenstierna. Oxenstierna had been a trusted aide to Christina's father. He often ran the government's affairs when Gustavus Adolphus was away at war.

Once a year, Christina stood before Oxenstierna and the other regents. They quizzed her on everything she had studied. She was scared to stand in front of the group of men and answer questions. But Christina did well in all her exams. Everyone agreed that Christina was very smart for a little girl.

When Christina wasn't studying, she rode her horses on the royal grounds. Many long afternoons were spent racing around a nearby lake. She was also a good hunter. A French ambassador once said Christina could "hit a running hare faster than any man."

ROYAL FEASTS

Christina often attended court ceremonies and banquets. A royal banquet included many different foods. The menu for a typical Christmas feast included fish, roast pig, eel pies, oysters, and many different sweets. The centerpiece of the meal was often a roast swan. The cooked meat would be decorated with the swan's feathers. It looked like the swan was alive and sitting in the middle of the table.

Christina enjoyed riding her horse across palace grounds with her dogs and servants.

4

Christina's
RULE

On Christina's 18th birthday, she assumed her full duties and power as queen. The regents were no longer in charge. Some of them, including Axel Oxenstierna, helped her run the government. But Christina had her own ideas of how she wanted to rule the country.

One of the first things Christina did was look for a way to end the Thirty Years' War. Christina knew that the war was bad for Sweden. Many men had died. The war was also very expensive. Sweden's people did not have enough money or food. She appointed two **delegates** to make peace arrangements with other governments. In 1648, Christina's efforts helped lead to the Treaty of Westphalia. The Thirty Years' War was finally over.

At age 18, Christina was officially crowned queen of Sweden.

delegate — someone who represents other people at a meeting

19

> "It is necessary to try to surpass one's self always; this occupation ought to last as long as life."
>
> Christina, explaining the importance of education

CHOOSING AN HEIR

The councilors disagreed with Christina on many matters. Some of Christina's councilors did not want to end the war. They hoped a longer war would eventually mean more land and a Protestant victory. Most of all, they fought with her about getting married. The council insisted that Christina get married and produce an heir.

However, Christina was not sure she wanted to get married. Getting married would mean sharing her crown. Christina also did not want to have children. When her councilors asked her about this, she told them, "I shall never marry." Christina named her cousin Charles X Gustav as her heir. The Riksdag members weren't happy, but they had to honor the queen's decision.

Christina enjoyed listening to René Descartes (standing at right).

Christina worked hard to make her court a center of learning. She started a library and the country's first newspaper. She also invited scholars from other countries to come to Sweden. One of these scholars was a Frenchman named René Descartes. Descartes was one of the most respected and well-known philosophers of his time. He came to Sweden and shared his ideas with Christina. While in Sweden, Descartes became very sick. He died there in 1650.

Although Christina's court was a center of learning, there were very few educational opportunities in Sweden. Sweden had just one university. The school didn't have enough money to run properly.

AN UNHAPPY QUEEN

Christina was especially interested in religion. She was a Lutheran, but she was curious about Roman Catholicism. The Swedish people were shocked and upset that their queen wanted to learn about another religion. As Christina learned more about Catholicism, she felt this religion best fit her beliefs.

Christina also realized that being the queen of Sweden didn't really make her happy. There were just too many things she wasn't allowed to do. She also feared she had disappointed her country by refusing to marry or produce an heir. She wanted Sweden to have a successful ruler. She realized she was not ready for the challenge. In 1654, Christina made a historic decision. She announced that she was going to **abdicate** the throne. Charles X Gustav would take over the throne.

At first, Charles (center) did not want to be Christina's successor.

abdicate — to give up power

Religions in Europe after the Reformation

Catholic
Angelican
Lutheran
Reformed
Orthodox
Muslim

0   300 miles
0   300 kilometers

NORWAY

SWEDEN

SCOTLAND

IRELAND

DENMARK

North Sea

ENGLAND

NETHERLANDS

ATLANTIC OCEAN

HOLY ROMAN EMPIRE

POLAND

AUSTRIA

FRANCE

HUNGARY

Black Sea

PAPAL STATES

PORTUGAL

SPAIN

Mediterranean Sea

RELIGIOUS REFORMATION

Four hundred years ago, religion was a major part of everyday life. In the early 1500s, a movement called the Reformation swept across Europe. Wars were fought over religious beliefs.

During the Reformation, many countries began to follow the Protestant religions. Other countries followed the Catholic religion. Many of these countries created official religions. They made it a crime to believe in any other religion. During Christina's time in Sweden, being a Catholic was illegal.

5

AFTER
The Throne

After giving up the crown, Christina replaced her royal dresses with men's pants. She cut her long hair. Christina converted to Catholicism and changed her name to Maria Christina Alexandra. She left Sweden on horseback and headed to Rome, the center of the Catholic Church. The warm air of Rome pleased Christina. Sweden had been a dark, cold land. But Rome was an exciting place full of culture and opportunity.

While in Rome, Christina continued to learn. She studied science, religion, and the arts. She also opened an opera house in Rome and gave money to several composers. She wrote letters and essays defending groups who were discriminated against because of their religious beliefs.

After leaving Sweden, Christina cut her hair and began wearing men's clothes.

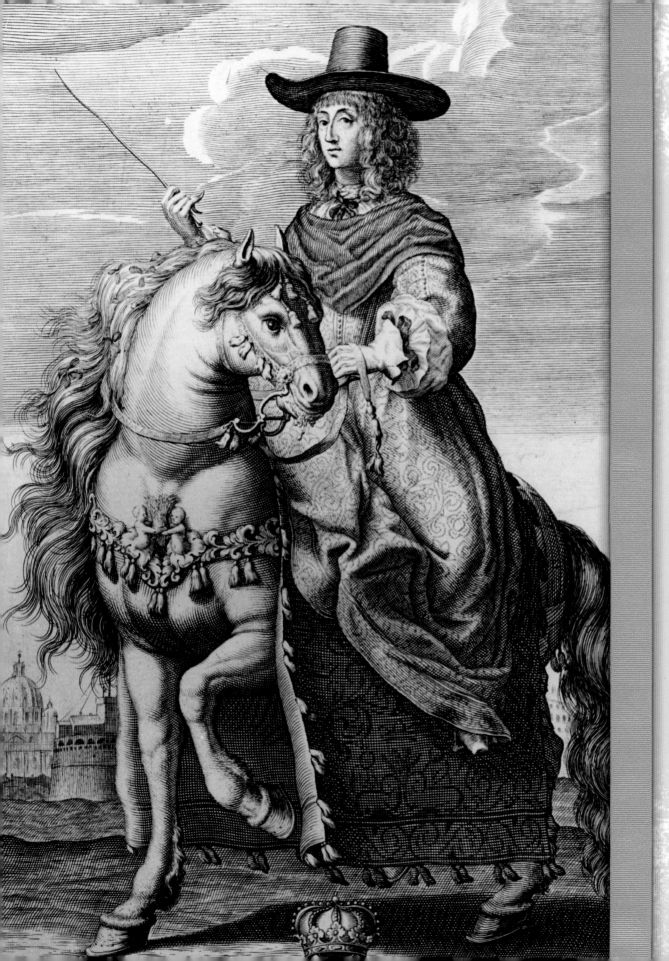

A NEW THRONE?

Though Christina had given up the Swedish crown, she still considered herself a queen. She believed she was born with the right to be a ruler.

Growing bored in Rome, Christina took an interest in foreign politics. In 1656, she plotted with French leaders to become Queen of Naples. But one of her servants, Marchese Gian-Rinaldo Monaldeschi, revealed her plot to officials in Naples. When Christina had him executed, her reputation was nearly ruined. After that, Christina gave up trying to be Queen of Naples. But it wouldn't be her last attempt at a throne.

When the king of Poland abdicated his throne, Christina hoped to be elected the new queen. This plan also failed. The noblemen in Poland decided they wanted a weak ruler who could be controlled. They knew they would not be able to control Christina.

After her second failed attempt at a crown, Christina stayed in Rome. Christina visited Sweden only a few times after abdicating her throne. During these trips, she never felt welcome in her homeland.

During the spring of 1689, Christina developed a fever. She battled it for weeks, but the illness left her weak. On April 19, 1689, at age 62, Christina died in Rome. She was dressed in a beautiful white gown covered in gold buttons and lace. Then she was brought to St. Peter's Church. This was a huge honor. Usually only men were buried there. Christina was also the first foreign ruler to be buried at St. Peter's.

Hundreds of people mourned Christina's death.

CHRISTINA ON THE BIG SCREEN

Swedish-born film star Greta Garbo starred in the 1933 film *Queen Christina*. Many film critics consider this Garbo's best performance.

While the film was very popular, it was only loosely based on Christina's life. Many of the events in the movie didn't really happen. The film focuses on a relationship between Christina and a Spanish ambassador. In the film, she abdicates the throne so that she can marry the ambassador. In real life, Christina never planned to marry. She left Sweden so she could practice the Catholic religion, not because of love.

A MISUNDERSTOOD QUEEN

Christina's court was a fascinating place. During a time when there were many unfair rules against women, Christina insisted on things done her way. For this reason, she was often criticized.

Staying true to herself and her beliefs made Christina's life uncomfortable. She put her own personal desires and freedom before duty to her country. This might sound selfish, but Christina also chose an heir who helped Sweden in ways she never could. More than 300 years later, she's still remembered as a misunderstood ruler who never stopped searching for a kingdom.

Christina will always be considered one of Sweden's most interesting rulers.

Glossary

abdicate (AB-di-kate) — to give up power

alliance (uh-LY-uhnts) — an agreement between groups
to work together

Catholic (KATH-uh-lik) — a member of the Roman Catholic Church

convert (kuhn-VURT) — to change religion

delegate (DEL-uh-guht) — someone who represents other people
at a meeting

heir (AIR) — someone who will become king or queen when the
current ruler dies

parliament (PAR-luh-muhnt) — a group of people who make laws
and run the government in some countries

philosopher (fuh-LOSS-uh-fer) — a person who studies truth
and knowledge

philosophy (fuh-LOSS-uh-fee) — the study of truth
and knowledge

Protestant (PROT-uh-stuhnt) — a Christian who does not belong
to the Roman Catholic or the Orthodox Church

regent (REE-jent) — a person who rules a country when the queen
or king is too young to do so

succeed (suhk-SEED) — to take over from someone in an
important position

Read More

Boraas, Tracey. *Sweden.* Countries and Cultures. Mankato, Minn.: Capstone Press, 2003.

Cotter, Charis. *Kids Who Rule: The Remarkable Lives of Five Child Monarchs.* Buffalo, N.Y.: Annick Press, 2007.

Kraske, Robert. *Queen Elizabeth I of England.* Queens and Princesses. Mankato, Minn.: Capstone Press, 2009.

Internet Sites

FactHound offers a safe, fun way to find educator-approved Internet sites related to this book.

Here's what you do:

1. Visit *www.facthound.com*
2. Choose your grade level.
3. Begin your search.

This book's ID number is 9781429623100.

FactHound will fetch the best sites for you!

Index